D1376713

COUNTRY PROFILES

GREECE

BY CHRISTINA LEAF

BELLWETHER MEDIA • MINNEAPOLIS, MN

Blastoff! Discovery launches a new mission: reading to learn. Filled with facts and features, each book offers you an exciting new world to explore!

This edition first published in 2020 by Bellwether Media, Inc.

No part of this publication may be reproduced in whole or in part without written permission of the publisher.
For information regarding permission, write to Bellwether Media, Inc., Attention: Permissions Department,
6012 Blue Circle Drive, Minnetonka, MN 55343.

Library of Congress Cataloging-in-Publication Data

Names: Leaf, Christina, author.
Title: Greece / by Christina Leaf.
Description: Minneapolis, MN : Bellwether Media, Inc., 2020. | Series: Blastoff! Discovery: Country Profiles | Includes bibliographical references and index. | Audience: Ages 7-13.
Identifiers: LCCN 2019001505 (print) | LCCN 2019002132 (ebook) | ISBN 9781618915900 (ebook) | ISBN 9781644870495 (hardcover : alk. paper)
Subjects: LCSH: Greece–Juvenile literature.
Classification: LCC DF717 (ebook) | LCC DF717 .L43 2020 (print) | DDC 949.5–dc23
LC record available at https://lccn.loc.gov/2019001505

Editor: Rebecca Sabelko   Designer: Brittany McIntosh

Printed in the United States of America, North Mankato, MN.

TABLE OF CONTENTS

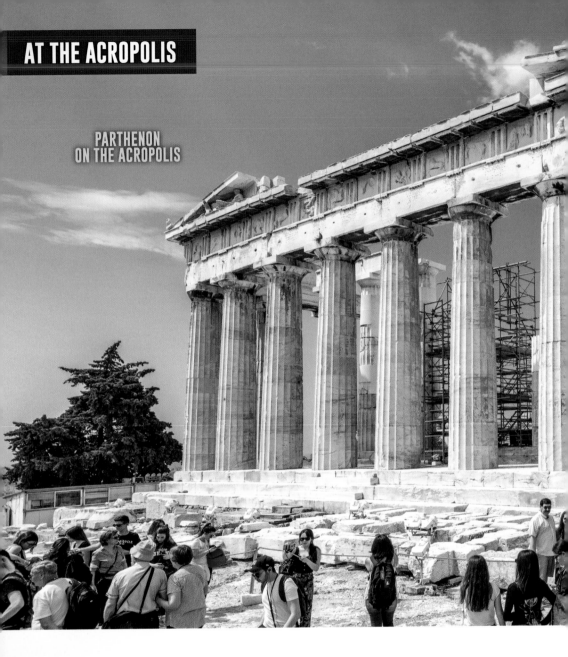

AT THE ACROPOLIS

PARTHENON
ON THE ACROPOLIS

A family walks up to the Acropolis. Its monuments
stand high above the city of Athens. At the top of the hill,
everyone admires the marble pillars of the Parthenon.
Then they wander among the other nearby temple ruins
that honor ancient gods and goddesses.

OTHER TOP SITES

DELPHI

MOUNT OLYMPUS

PALACE OF KNOSSOS

SANTORINI

SURPRISE!

The ruins of the ancient city of Athens were found as workers were planning for the Acropolis Museum. They had to make new plans to include them!

In the afternoon, the family escapes the heat by visiting the Acropolis Museum. Pottery and sculptures that are thousands of years old line the walls. From a balcony, they look down at ruins from ancient Athens. Even in modern times, Greece's history is proudly on display!

BULGARIA

NORTH
MACEDONIA

THESSALONIKI

ALBANIA

GREECE

AEGEAN
SEA

IONIAN
SEA

PATRAS

ATHENS

MEDITERRANEAN
SEA

NOT GREEK TO THEM

Greeks call their country Hellas in their language. The name "Greece" was the Roman name of the country. However, research suggests that "Graiko" was an ancient name for early peoples of Greece.

TURKEY

Greece lies along the Mediterranean Sea in southeastern Europe. Most of the country's 50,949 square miles (131,957 square kilometers) are on the Balkan **Peninsula**. Greece's capital, Athens, sits on the southeastern end of the **mainland**. The rest of the country is scattered across more than 2,000 islands.

Albania, North Macedonia, and Bulgaria border Greece to the north. A small part of Turkey touches Greece in the northeast. The Aegean Sea lies to the east of Greece's mainland. The Ionian Sea lines Greece's western coast.

N W E S

Mountains shape much of Greece's land. The forested Rhodope Mountains line the northeastern border. They flatten into low **plains** by the northeastern coast. Snaking down the center of the country are the Pindus Mountains. In the south, the Peloponnese peninsula is mountainous with some forests. Most of Greece's islands are rocky and covered in hills.

N
W —┼— E
S

■ = PINDUS MOUNTAINS   ■ = PELOPONNESE PENINSULA

■ = RHODOPE MOUNTAINS

PELOPONNESE PENINSULA

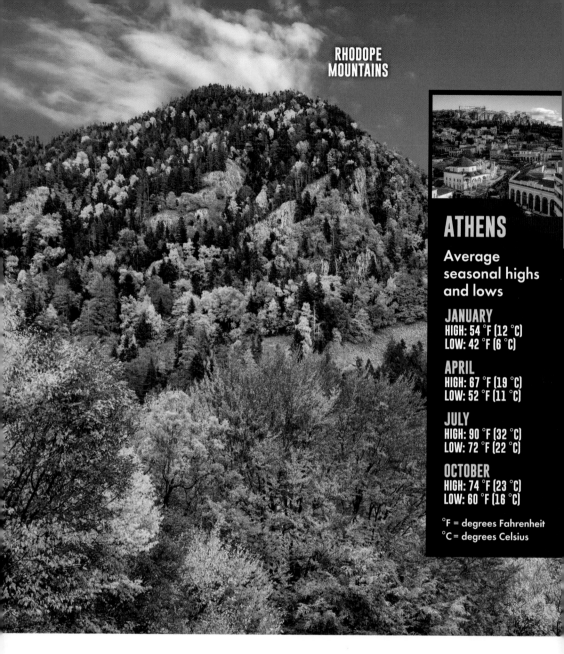

ATHENS

**Average
seasonal highs
and lows**

JANUARY
HIGH: 54 °F (12 °C)
LOW: 42 °F (6 °C)

APRIL
HIGH: 67 °F (19 °C)
LOW: 52 °F (11 °C)

JULY
HIGH: 90 °F (32 °C)
LOW: 72 °F (22 °C)

OCTOBER
HIGH: 74 °F (23 °C)
LOW: 60 °F (16 °C)

°F = degrees Fahrenheit
°C = degrees Celsius

Because of its southern location by the sea, Greece has a
Mediterranean climate. Winters are mild and rainy, while
summers are hot and dry. Areas in the mountains are cooler
and may see snow in winter.

Greece's different regions hold many types of animals. Wildcats and brown bears roam through the mountains, alongside martens and roe deer. Leopard snakes and tortoises prefer dry **scrubland**. Rare wild goats called kri-kris wander the island of Crete. The surrounding seas hold creatures like octopuses, squids, and dolphins, Greece's national animal.

Raptors such as the booted eagle soar above the country. Butterflies, once honored by the ancient Greeks, also take to the skies. Greece welcomes many **migrating** birds, including geese and kestrels.

EUROPEAN WILDCAT

COMMON TORTOISE

LEOPARD SNAKE

LESSER KESTREL

RARE BIRDS

Many people consider the phoenix to be Greece's national animal. Stories of this mythological bird say that the birds do not die. Instead, they burst into flames and are reborn from the ashes.

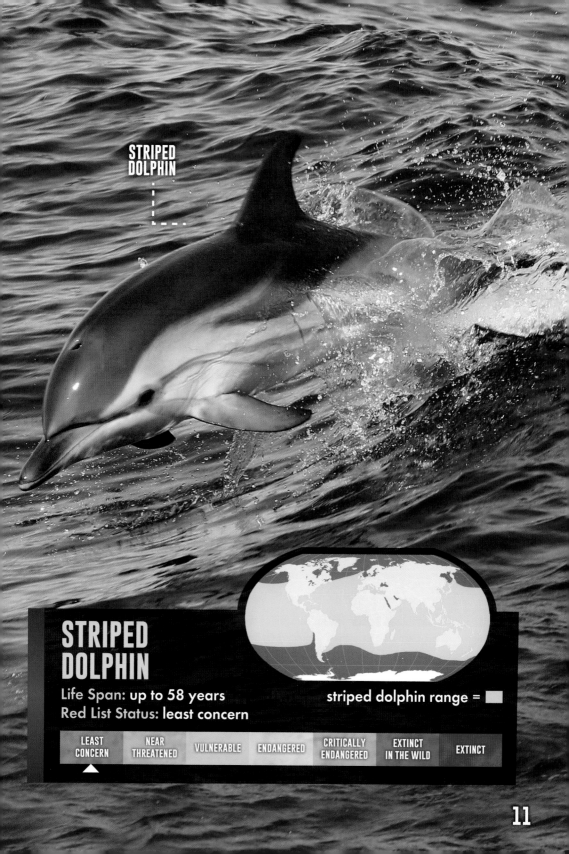

STRIPED
DOLPHIN

STRIPED
DOLPHIN

Life Span: up to 58 years
Red List Status: least concern

striped dolphin range = ▮

LEAST CONCERN	NEAR THREATENED	VULNERABLE	ENDANGERED	CRITICALLY ENDANGERED	EXTINCT IN THE WILD	EXTINCT
▲						

Most people in Greece are Greek. However, some people identify with other **ethnic** groups, including Albanians, Turks, and Roma. Recently, many **refugees** have traveled through Greece seeking safety throughout Europe.

Almost all Greeks belong to the Church of Greece, which is part of the Eastern Orthodox Church. Other Greeks are Muslim or Catholic. Greek is the official language of the country. The language has been around for thousands of years, but people speak a modern form today.

FAMOUS FACE

Name: **Arianna Huffington**
Birthday: **July 15, 1950**
Hometown: **Athens, Greece**
Famous for: **The author of 15 books, a founder of the Huffington Post web site, and the creator and CEO of the health and wellness company, Thrive Global**

SPEAK GREEK

Greek uses the Greek alphabet. However, Greek words can be written with the English alphabet so you can read them.

ENGLISH	GREEK	HOW TO SAY IT
hello	ya soo	YAH soo
goodbye	adeeo	ah-DEE-oh
please	parakalo	pah-rah-kah-LO
thank you	efkharisto	eff-har-ee-STOW
yes	neh	neh
no	okhee	OH-hee

ATHENS

Most Greeks live in cities on the coast or on the plains. People generally live in modern apartment buildings. Older sections of cities have short stone buildings. **Rural** house styles vary by area and may be concrete or stone. Cities have modern public transit, and paved roads and railroads connect much of the country. Ferries move people between islands.

THESSALONIKI

BIRTHPLACE OF DEMOCRACY

Athens was the first place to have a democratic society. This form of government, ruled by the people, is the foundation of many countries today.

Greek communities are close-knit, especially in rural villages. Families live close to one another when possible. Kids may stay with their parents into adulthood until they find jobs. They care for elderly parents later in life.

Hospitality has had a strong influence on Greek **culture** since ancient times. The Greeks are welcoming and generous to visitors. They open up their homes and insist on sharing food and drinks with guests.

Leisure time is important to the Greeks. In small towns and villages, it is common to take an evening walk. People stroll down main street or along the shore and chat with friends. In some places, the workday pauses for a midday break. People rest, share lunch with family, and stay out of the hot Mediterranean sun.

SHOWERING WITH LUCK

An old Greek tradition says spitting on people brings them luck! It is said to ward off evil spirits. Today, most people make the noise but spit only a tiny bit.

The Greeks are very proud of their educational system. All public schools are free. Children start school at age 6 and must attend school until age 15. Many continue with more high school afterward. Languages are an important part of schooling. Students learn Greek, English, and another European language.

Most Greeks work in **service jobs**. They own small businesses or work in the government or **tourism**. Factory workers make metals, medicine, and fabrics. On small farms, a few Greeks raise crops such as olives, grapes, and tomatoes. Some raise goats and sheep. Fishing is also an important industry.

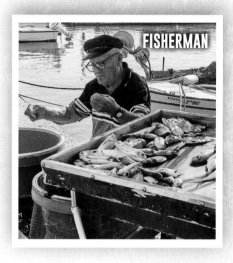

FISHERMAN

GOAT FARMER

KITESURFING

The national sport of Greece is soccer, but basketball is also popular. Gymnastics and track and field have deep roots in Greek culture as well. The country's clear water is perfect for swimming, sailing, and kitesurfing. The mountains offer great hikes, and in the winter, many places to ski.

GYMNASTICS

Kids like skateboarding and biking in cities. Adults may meet friends at coffee shops to chat or play backgammon. In summer, Greeks relax outdoors at cafés. They may also catch a play at an outdoor theater.

CAFÉ

BEAN MOSAICS

What You Need:
- glue
- paintbrushes
- cardboard
- a variety of dried beans in different colors (peas, lentils, kidney beans, etc.)
- a pencil

Instructions:
1. Draw a design on the cardboard.
2. Paint glue on a small part of the cardboard.
3. Put different colored beans on the area with glue.
4. Repeat for the whole design.

MEZE TABLES

Greeks love to gather at tables with *mezes*, or small plates, to enjoy each other's company. Dips like *tzatziki* or *taramasalata* served with pita bread are popular. Some mezes are as simple as olives.

Greece's climate allows for a large variety of foods. Olives are present at most meals, and olive oil is a key ingredient in cooking. Garlic and lemon flavor many dishes, too. Seafood from the coasts includes octopus, squid, and shrimp.

Greek breakfasts are often yogurt and honey with fruit, or a cheese pastry. *Gyros* and grilled *souvlaki* are favorite street snacks. Dinner is usually the main meal. **Traditional** dishes include roast lamb, stuffed grape leaves, and *moussaka*, an eggplant dish. Village salads, made of tomatoes, cucumbers, onions, and feta cheese, accompany meals. *Baklava* and other desserts are often covered in honey.

GYRO

MOUSSAKA

TZATZIKI RECIPE

Ingredients:
1 cup plain Greek yogurt
1 cucumber, grated and drained
2 cloves garlic, minced
1 tablespoon lemon juice
2 tablespoons dill
Salt and pepper to taste

Steps:
1. Combine ingredients in a medium bowl. Chill.
2. Serve as a dip with pita bread or veggies!

Holy Week and Easter are Greece's biggest celebrations. As Orthodox Christians, Greeks celebrate later than other Christians. On Good Friday, Greeks walk through the streets and scatter flowers. At midnight on Easter Sunday, fireworks and loud drums echo through the night. The following day, people attend church and eat a lunch of roast lamb.

GOOD FRIDAY

INDEPENDENCE DAY

Greeks celebrate Independence Day on March 25. Athens has a big military parade. In smaller towns, children march through the streets, waving flags while dressed in traditional Greek clothing.

Christmas is another important holiday. Special breads and cookies grace the feast tables, while trees and angels decorate houses. Traditionally, people open presents on New Year's Day, which Greeks celebrate as the feast of St. Basil. Even in modern times, Greeks hold the traditions of their ancient country dear!

480 BCE

Greece enters into a golden age of power, wealth, and influence

146 BCE

Romans take control of the country, ending the ancient Greek Empire

AROUND 3000 BCE

The Minoan civilization on Crete is the first major civilization in the area that is now Greece

1453

The Roman Empire falls to the Ottoman Empire, which takes control of Greece

700s BCE

The Greek alphabet is created

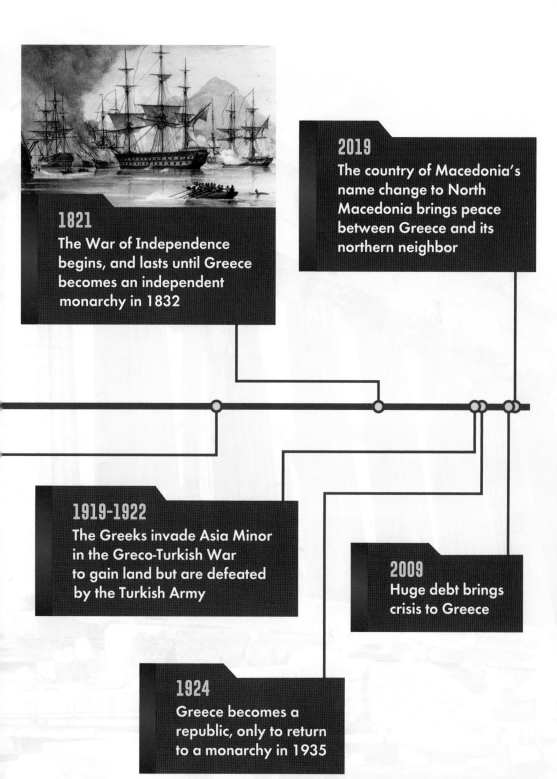

1821
The War of Independence begins, and lasts until Greece becomes an independent monarchy in 1832

2019
The country of Macedonia's name change to North Macedonia brings peace between Greece and its northern neighbor

1919-1922
The Greeks invade Asia Minor in the Greco-Turkish War to gain land but are defeated by the Turkish Army

2009
Huge debt brings crisis to Greece

1924
Greece becomes a republic, only to return to a monarchy in 1935

GREECE FACTS

Official Name: Hellenic Republic

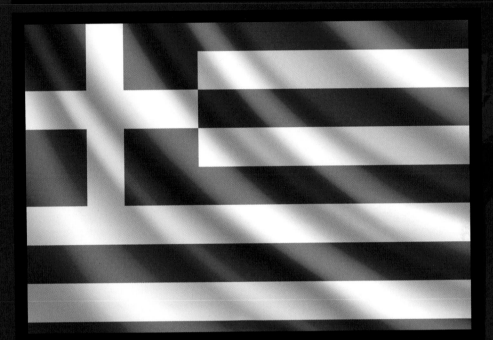

Flag of Greece: The Greek flag has nine stripes of blue and white that alternate. In the upper left corner is a blue square with a white cross in the middle. This cross stands for the Greek Orthodox Church. The color of blue is not set. It has changed back and forth from light blue to a darker shade over the years.

Area: 50,949 square miles
(131,957 square kilometers)

Capital City: Athens

Important Cities: Thessaloniki, Patras

Population:
10,761,523 (July 2018)

COUNTRYSIDE
20.9%

WHERE
PEOPLE LIVE

CITY
79.1%

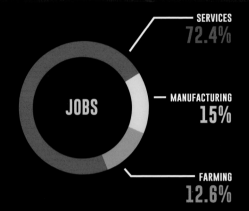

JOBS

SERVICES
72.4%

MANUFACTURING
15%

FARMING
12.6%

Main Exports:

olives   meat   beverages

chemicals   textiles

National Holiday:
Independence Day (March 25)

Main Language:
Greek

Form of Government:
parliamentary republic

Title for Country Leaders:
president (head of state),
prime minister (head of government)

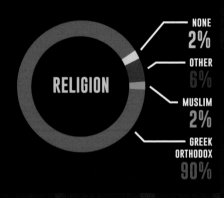

RELIGION

NONE
2%

OTHER
6%

MUSLIM
2%

GREEK
ORTHODOX
90%

Unit of Money:
euro

GLOSSARY

culture—the beliefs, arts, and ways of life in a place or society

ethnic—related to a group of people who share customs and an identity

hospitality—a generous and friendly way of treating guests

leisure—free time

mainland—a continent or main part of a country

migrating—traveling from one place to another, often with the seasons

peninsula—a section of land that extends out from a larger piece of land and is almost completely surrounded by water

plains—large areas of flat land

refugees—people who flee their country for safety

rural—related to the countryside

scrubland—dry land that has mostly low plants and few trees

service jobs—jobs that perform tasks for people or businesses

tourism—the business of people traveling to visit other places

traditional—related to customs, ideas, or beliefs handed down from one generation to the next

TO LEARN MORE

AT THE LIBRARY

Dickmann, Nancy. *Ancient Greece*. Mankato, Minn.: Capstone Press, 2017.

Napoli, Donna Jo. *Treasury of Greek Mythology: Classic Stories of Gods, Goddesses, Heroes, and Monsters*. Washington, D.C.: National Geographic Society, 2011.

Tabachnik, Anna T. *Greece*. New York, N.Y.: Scholastic, 2019.

ON THE WEB

FACTSURFER

Factsurfer.com gives you a safe, fun way to find more information.

1. Go to www.factsurfer.com.

2. Enter "Greece" into the search box and click Q.

3. Select your book cover to see a list of related web sites.

INDEX